I0828201

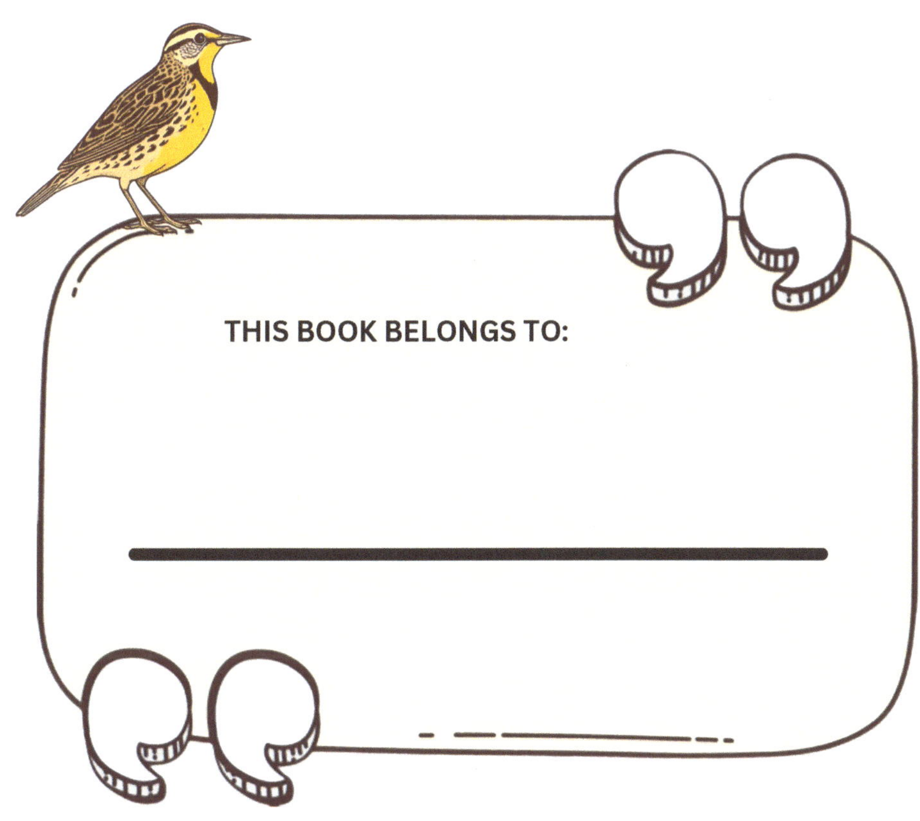
THIS BOOK BELONGS TO:

WELCOME
TO OREGON
OF OREGON
THE UNION
1859

Dedicated to all the explorers.

ISBN 978-1-970416-01-5

www.joeysavestheday.com

Mimi Books™ Publishing

A Mimi Book

Oregon got its name from the early explorers and maps that described the region long before it became a state. The exact origin of the word "Oregon" is still debated, but many believe it may have come from an old term referring to the beautiful rivers in the area. Over time, the name Oregon became widely used, and it eventually became the official name of the state we know today.

Eastern Oregon

explore

Oregon has a long history that begins with Native American nations who lived among its forests, rivers, mountains, and coastline for thousands of years. Tribes such as the Chinook, Klamath, Nez Perce, and Umatilla built strong communities across the region. In the 1800s, explorers, fur traders, and later settlers arrived, many traveling along the famous Oregon Trail.

Oregon was the thirty-third state to join the Union. It officially became a state on February 14, 1859.

Oregon is located in the Pacific Northwest region of the United States. It is bordered by Washington, Idaho, Nevada, and California, and it also touches the Pacific Ocean along its western coast.

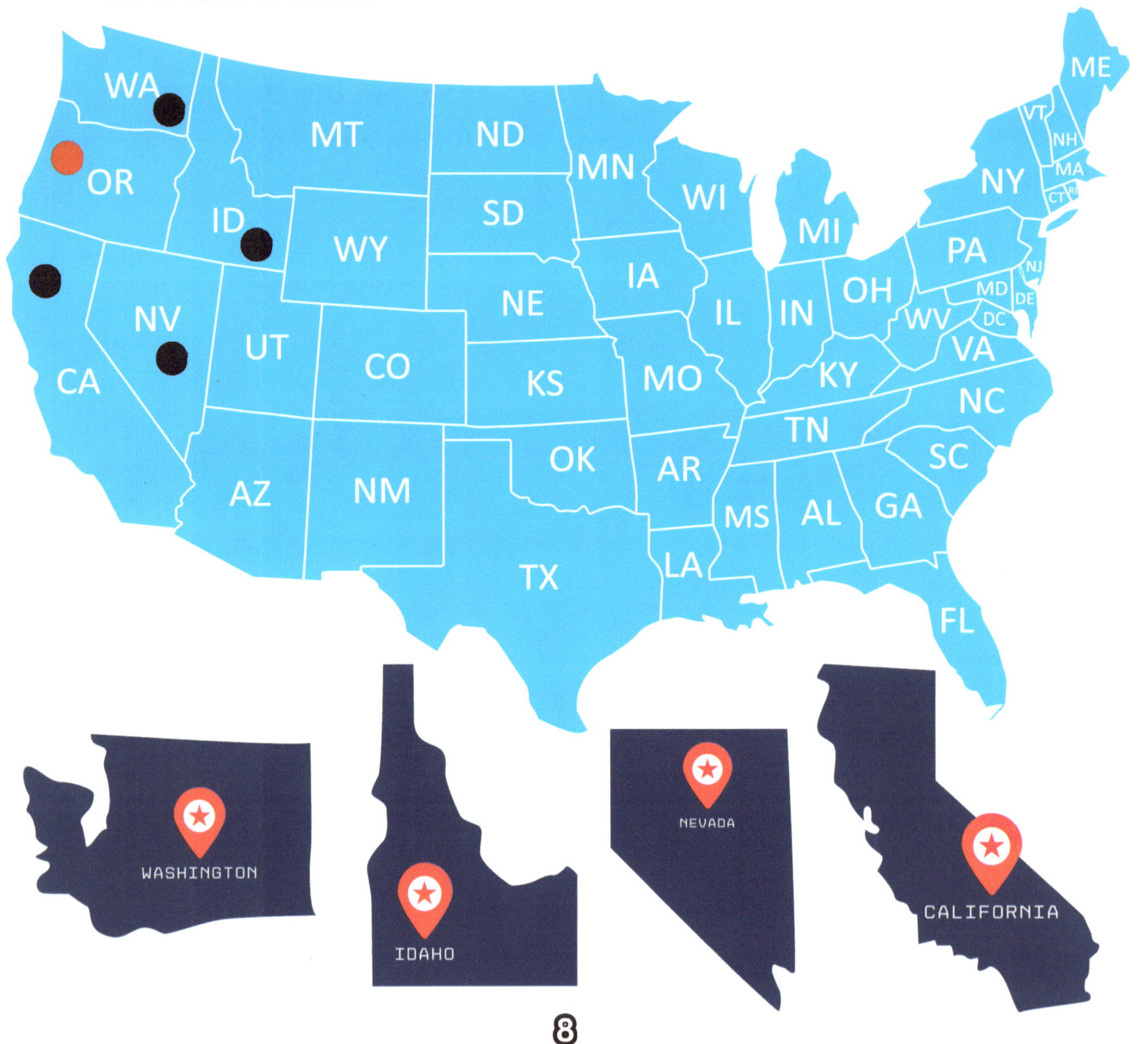

Salem is the capital of Oregon, and it officially became the state capital in 1859.

Salem, Oregon, has an estimated population of about 180,000 people.

Oregon is the ninth largest state in the United States by area.

Bend, Oregon

There are approximately 4,273,000 people residing in the state of Oregon.

Eugene, Oregon

Lewis and Clark, two famous explorers of the American West, are remembered at Fort Clatsop near Astoria, Oregon. This wooden fort is a careful replica of the place where the Corps of Discovery spent the winter of 1805–1806 after reaching the Pacific Ocean. The rooms are filled with simple tools, maps, and supplies that show what life was like during their long journey.

Captains Lewis & Clark holding a Council with the Indians

Meriwether Lewis

William Clark

Oregon is known for its delicious marionberries! These juicy, dark-purple berries were created in Oregon and grow especially well in the state's rich soil. Marionberries are sweet, tangy, and perfect for pies, jams, and summertime treats.

OREGON

There are 36 counties in Oregon.

Here is a list of twenty of those counties:

Baker	Coos	Gilliam	Umatilla
Benton	Crook	Grant	Union
Clackamas	Curry	Harney	Wallowa
Clatsop	Deschutes	Hood River	Wasco
Columbia	Douglas	Jackson	Washington

South Falls is one of Oregon's most famous waterfalls, dropping in a long, bright curtain of water. A special trail lets kids walk behind the falls, where they can hear the roar and feel the cool mist. The canyon was shaped by lava and rushing water long ago, creating the smooth rock walls around it. In spring the waterfall is powerful, and in winter icy patterns sparkle along the cliff.

Silver Falls State Park

Oregon Trail

One of the most important moments in Oregon's history is the arrival of thousands of pioneers along the Oregon Trail in the mid-1800s. This long and challenging journey brought families, farmers, and dreamers across the continent to settle in the fertile Willamette Valley. Their arrival helped small settlements grow into thriving communities and played a major role in shaping Oregon's early development.

The Yaquina Bay Bridge is a historic landmark that stretches across Yaquina Bay in Newport, Oregon. Completed in 1936, this beautiful green arch bridge is one of the most famous along the Oregon Coast and is known for its graceful Art Deco design!

The Oregon state bird is the Western Meadowlark. It was chosen as the state bird in 1927.

The official state flower of Oregon is the Oregon Grape. It was chosen as the state flower in 1899.
OFFICIAL
OFFICIAL
OFFICIAL

Oregon's nickname is the Beaver State.

THE

ST8

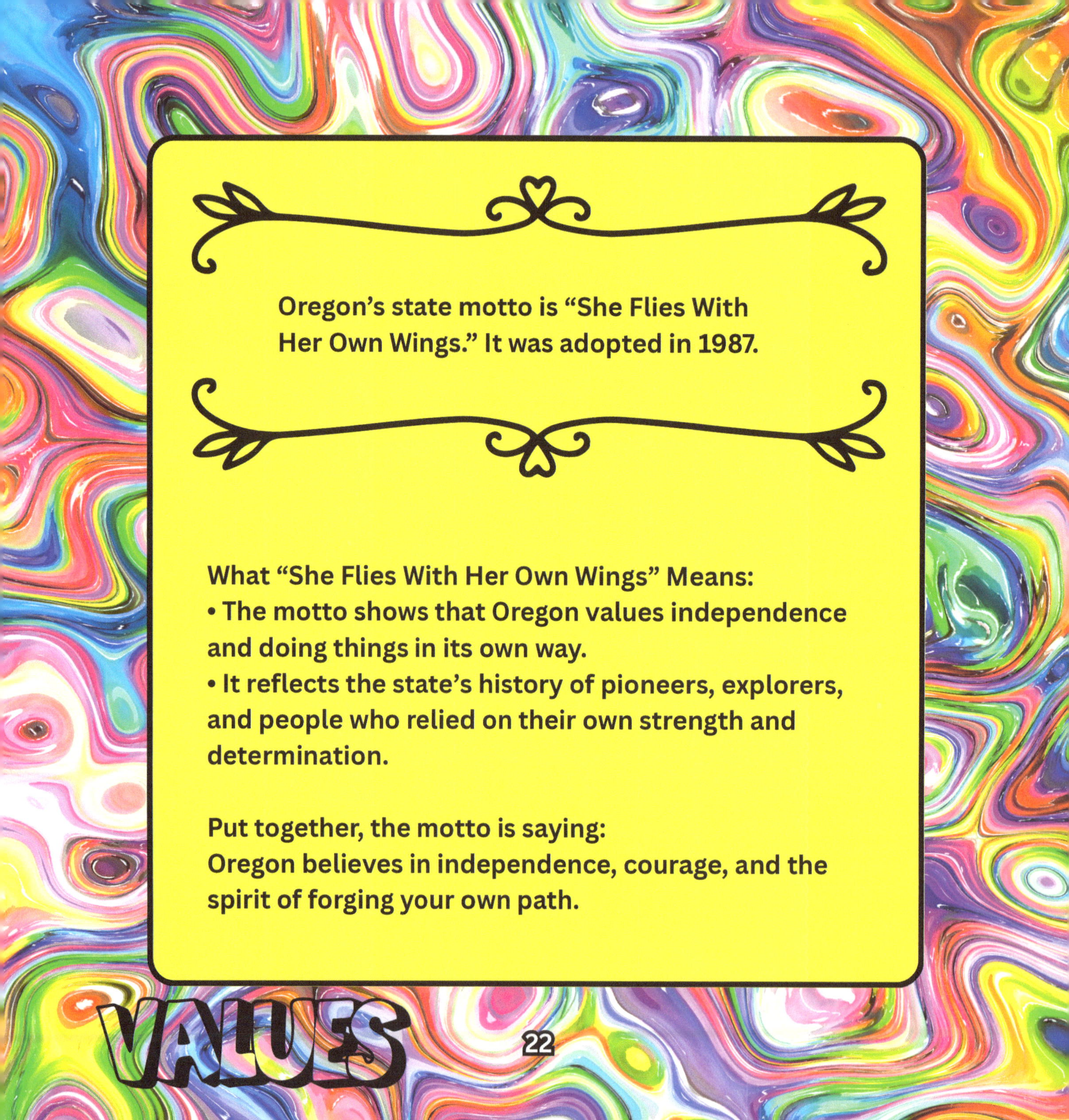

Oregon's state motto is "She Flies With Her Own Wings." It was adopted in 1987.

What "She Flies With Her Own Wings" Means:
- The motto shows that Oregon values independence and doing things in its own way.
- It reflects the state's history of pioneers, explorers, and people who relied on their own strength and determination.

Put together, the motto is saying:
Oregon believes in independence, courage, and the spirit of forging your own path.

The abbreviation for Oregon is OR.

OR

Oregon's state flag was officially adopted in 1925.

1859

Some crops grown in Oregon are berries, pears, hazelnuts, and potatoes.

Some animals that live in Oregon are Roosevelt elk, gray wolves, porcupines, raccoons, and osprey.

Oregon experiences a wide range of temperatures throughout the year. The hottest temperature ever recorded in the state was 119 degrees Fahrenheit, measured in Pelton Dam on June 29, 2021. In contrast, the coldest temperature documented was −54 degrees Fahrenheit, recorded in Seneca on February 10, 1933.

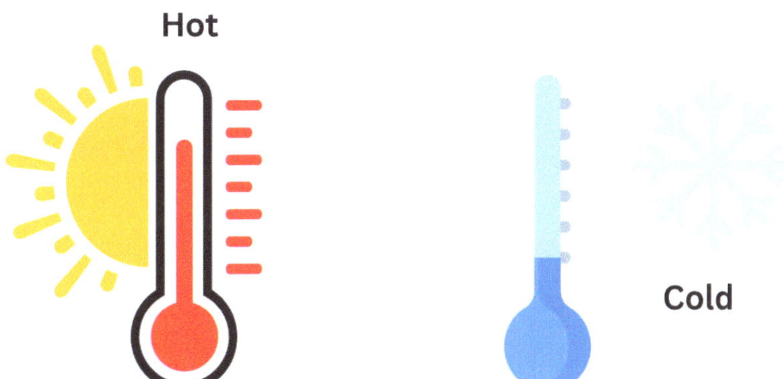

The Oregon Zoo in Portland is a wonderful place to explore, with animals from all around the world. Kids can see elephants, amur tigers, bears, African painted dogs, and playful primates, along with colorful birds and reptiles.

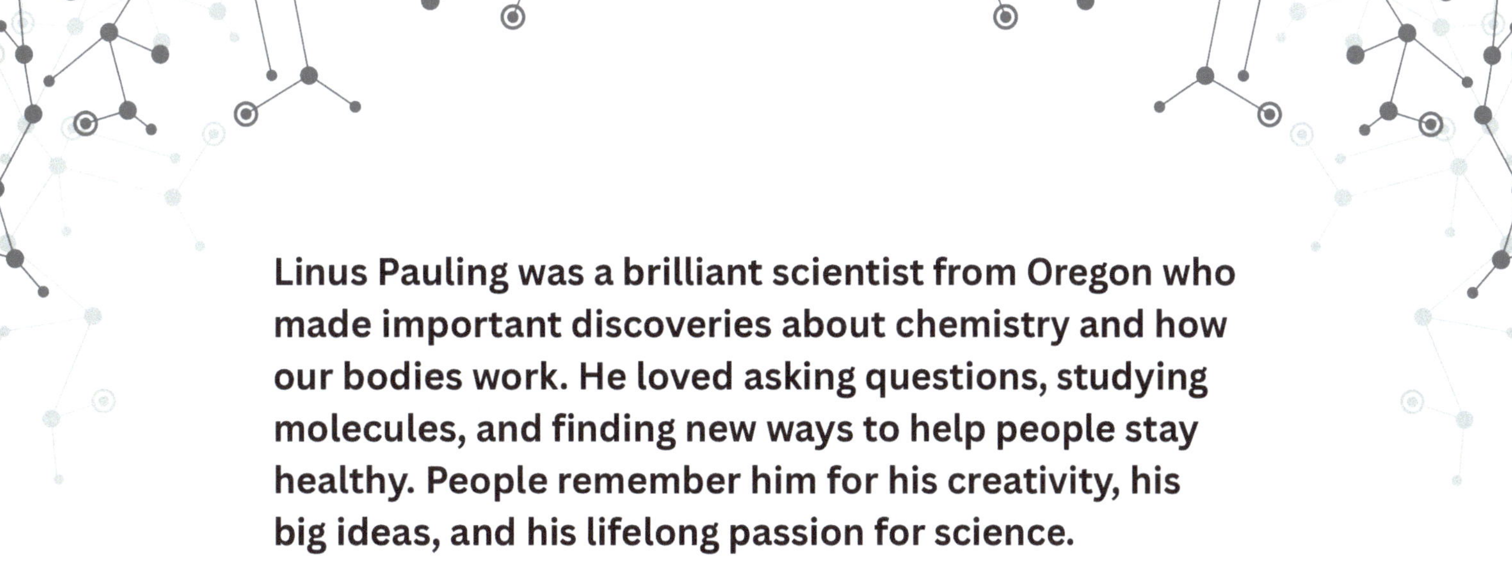

Linus Pauling was a brilliant scientist from Oregon who made important discoveries about chemistry and how our bodies work. He loved asking questions, studying molecules, and finding new ways to help people stay healthy. People remember him for his creativity, his big ideas, and his lifelong passion for science.

Stay healthy

The largest airport in Oregon is Portland International Airport, located in Portland. It sits at 7000 NE Airport Way and serves as the main travel hub for people flying in and out of Oregon. This airport connects travelers to cities all across the country and to destinations around the world, making it one of the busiest and most important airports in the Pacific Northwest.

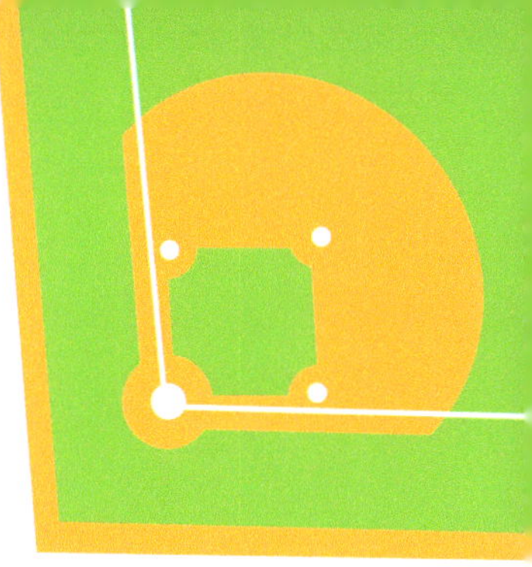

The Hillsboro Hops are a professional baseball team based in Hillsboro, a growing city in Oregon's Tualatin Valley. They play their home games at the new Hillsboro Hops Ballpark, located inside the Gordon Faber Recreation Complex. This bright and lively stadium is known for its fun atmosphere, friendly fans, and beautiful views of the surrounding hills. The Hops are part of Minor League Baseball, and many talented young players wear their uniform as they build their skills and work toward the major leagues.

FOOTBALL

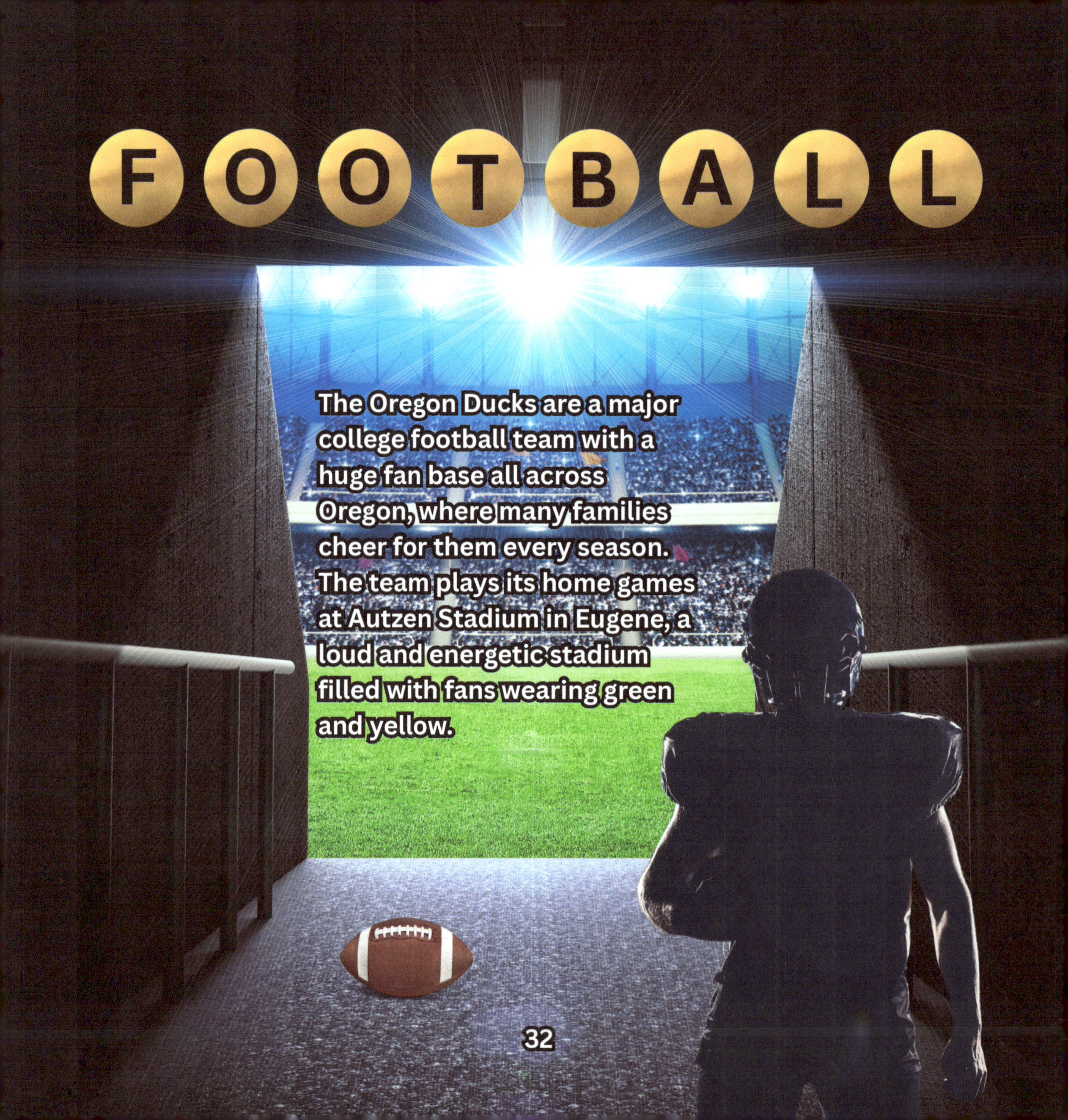

The Oregon Ducks are a major college football team with a huge fan base all across Oregon, where many families cheer for them every season. The team plays its home games at Autzen Stadium in Eugene, a loud and energetic stadium filled with fans wearing green and yellow.

The Douglas fir is Oregon's state tree. It's known for its tall, straight trunk and soft green needles that stay on the tree all year long. The Douglas fir was officially adopted as the state tree in 1939, and its strong wood and towering height have made it a beloved symbol of Oregon's forests and natural beauty.

The Chinook salmon is Oregon's state fish. It's a large, powerful fish known for its silver body and incredible strength as it swims through rivers and out to the Pacific Ocean. The Chinook salmon was officially adopted as the state fish in 1961, and its long migrations and importance to Oregon's rivers and wildlife make it a treasured symbol of the state's natural beauty.

Can you name these?

I hope you enjoyed learning about Oregon.

To explore fun facts about the other 49 states, visit my website at www.joeysavestheday.com. You'll also find a wide variety of homeschool resources to support joyful learning at home. If you enjoyed this book, I would be grateful if you left a review. Your feedback truly helps. Thank you for your support!

Check out these other interesting books in the
50 States Fact Books Series!

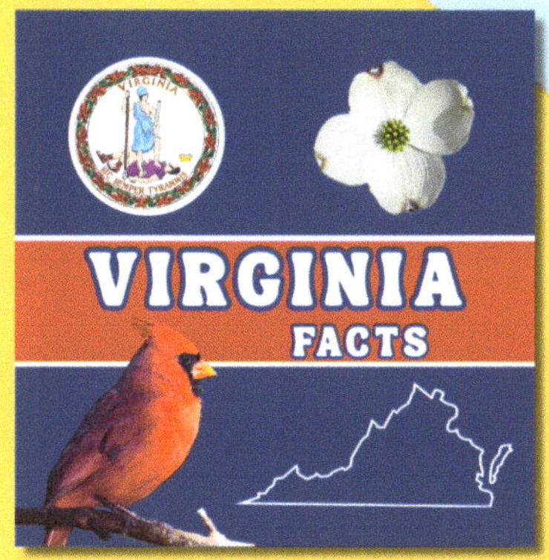

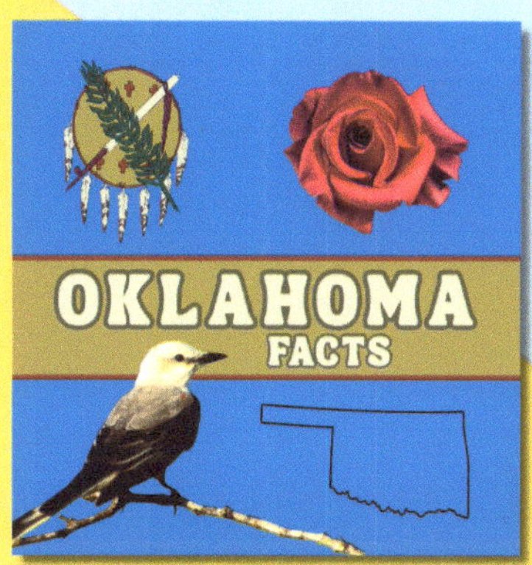

www.mimibooks.com